Life is Fine

Deardra Zahara Duncan
Illustrator: Kalila Ain Abdur-Razzaq

Life is Fine
Copyright © 2022 by Deardra Zahara Duncan & Kalila Ain Abdur-Razzaq

All rights reserved. No part of this publication may be reproduced, distributed, or transmitted in any form or by any means, including photocopying, recording, or other electronic or mechanical methods, without the prior written permission of the author, except in the case of brief quotations embodied in critical reviews and certain other non-commercial uses permitted by copyright law.

Tellwell Talent
www.tellwell.ca

ISBN
978-0-2288-4313-9 (Hardcover)
978-0-2288-4312-2 (Paperback)

Dedicated to the memory of my fathers
Mack Howard Duncan
and
Shelton Alkamal Duncan

Heartfelt Tribute to poet
Langston Hughes

Special Gratitude to…All Divine Forces; Olodumare, Orisha, Egun, Guides and Angels

Mom – who still reminds me that life is fine

Maxwell – for living shared experiences and being my Gibraltar

My adoring daughters, Princess Noni and Sweet Kalila – for your inspirations, honesty and constant affection

Extended Family & Friends for your encouragement, love and support in this wonderful life

This book is for the power in healing.

At bedtime, Daddy would say goodnight with a poem. Langston was my favorite. For a whole week I was obsessed with "*Life is Fine*," because my dad would sing it to me like a song. Each night we made it more jazzy and rhythmical and I would dance and feel happy. It was our special song. At the end of the poem, we'd shout, "Life is fine! Fine as wine! Life is fine!" and I would fall onto my bed laughing.

"You so fine my daddy!" I would beam.

"And you so fine my sweetie." He would say back. "Remember Dee Dee, you can always do what seems difficult when you believe in yourself and love life. If you do, everything will turn out just fine!"

Then we'd rub noses and kiss goodnight.

Mack Duncan was my daddy and he was the coolest man I knew.

On the weekend, I kept thinking about the poem and humming our tune. On Saturday, my sister Ramona made a bath that wasn't hot enough so I sang the part about going to the river bank and it being too cold to sink! She laughed and said, "Oh, how cute!"

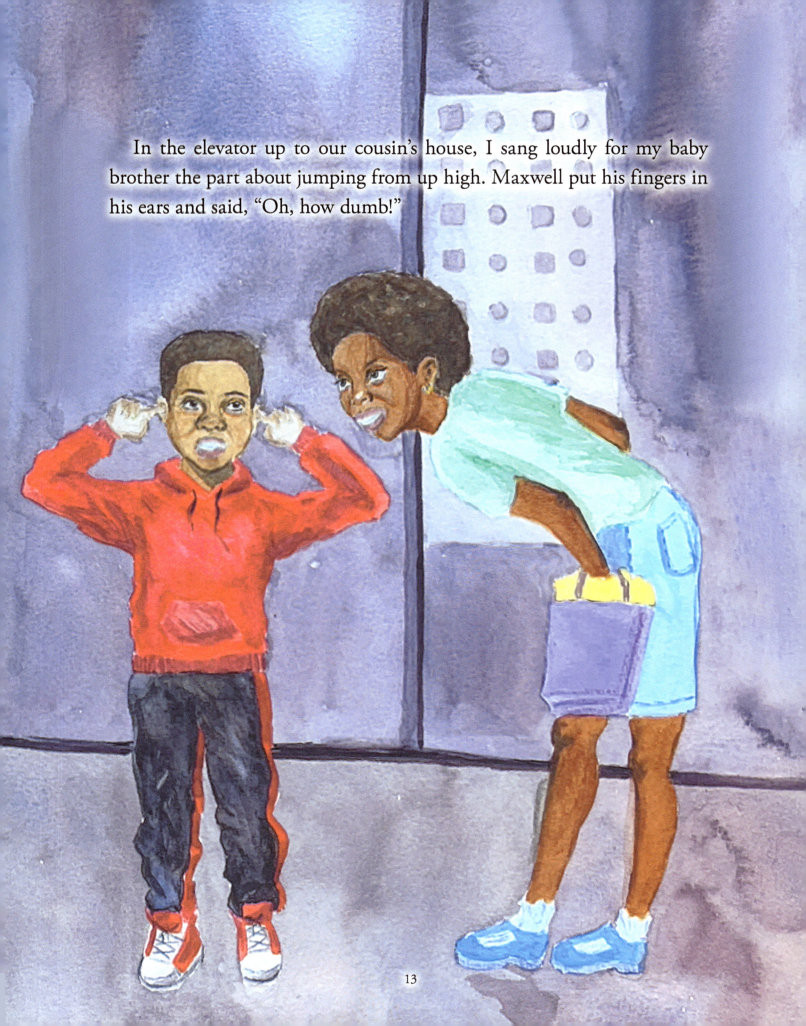

In the elevator up to our cousin's house, I sang loudly for my baby brother the part about jumping from up high. Maxwell put his fingers in his ears and said, "Oh, how dumb!"

Then, on Monday morning the poem was still with me! During math when everyone else was done, I still had four problems left. I couldn't concentrate because kids were yelling out, "FINISHED!" and slamming their books closed. Just when I thought I'd never get done, my brain hummed, *"life is fine, fine as wine"* and then I was completing the last problem!

In gym, I swung two strikes when my team had two outs. All the kids were shouting with ugly faces and making a big deal. I was confused and embarrassed and didn't want to strike out too. I took a deep breath and hummed *"life is fine"* I swung hard and hit a home run!

Later, in art class, Ms. Ichi was delighted when I sang for her our poem-song. She encouraged the class to paint "Life is Fine" pictures. After a while, the phone rang and Ms. Ichi told me to pack up because I was going home early. Luckily, I had just finished my beautiful painting. It was a watercolor of the river bank from the poem, with a bright rainbow, green trees, cotton clouds and colorful balloons floating up to the blue sky. I couldn't wait to show my dad!

I couldn't believe Auntie Dot was waiting to pick me up. She had never come to my school before. She said she had a surprise for me.

We went to the candy store and bought everything I wanted - bubble gum, sour balls, taffy, and candy bars! I couldn't believe how generous she was about all the sugar!

I was so happy. It felt like I was floating in the rainbow of my picture. I ate lots of sweets all the way home. Auntie Dot carried my artwork so it wouldn't get crushed and I let her hold my hand because I could tell she wanted to protect me.

When we arrived home Grandaddy, neighbors and my favorite uncle Persey, were in my house. My sister and brother were not there, and I wondered what was going on. Before I could speak to anyone, Auntie Dot came close to me and whispered,

"Your mother is in her room, Dee Dee. Go, she needs you." Just then, I noticed that my auntie and everybody else looked sad.

I felt scared, and knew something was wrong. From inside of me, the rainbow dropped away. I walked slowly to my parent's room. With each step the staircase grew longer and scarier.

I opened the door, and mom was sitting on her bed. When she looked at me, I could tell she had been crying. Her eyes were red and puffy, and she had balls of tissues on her bed. My big brother Kamal was standing by the window, and I was really shocked to see him since he lived far away. I ran into Mom's arms asking, "What's the matter Mommy, what?!" She hugged me tightly and began to cry. I felt small and helpless but wanted to make her feel better.

I searched my brother's face for an answer. He walked over and hugged us. Then he started saying serious words, "Something has happened, and I want you to be strong and listen closely as I speak to you okay? You are very loved." I sat next to mommy and nodded yes, but I didn't feel strong. I felt afraid.

"Life can be confusing. There are happy, wonderful times, and there are sad, hurtful times. No one knows why it is this way. For some important reason, God decided that we must feel all things, good and bad. What makes life difficult is having faith *inside* while living through the bad times. We have faith that the hurt will end so we may get to enjoy the good times that are waiting to happen."

"Life is born into the world but after a while, all life must end, like Grandma Lalee. A life can end when it is young or old, healthy or sickly. When it's time for our life to end, we must go. It doesn't mean we don't want to stay or that we don't love our family and friends anymore. It just means our time here is over and we must return to the special place we came from. Do you understand?" I said yes, because I did understand. Someone had died and gone to live beyond the sky. They would become the way I imagined my Grandma, like an angel watching over us. Somebody had died, but who was it?

My mother and brother's faces looked like they wanted to say sorry to me. "Dee Dee," my big brother said gently, "this morning our daddy returned to that special place." I flung my arms around his neck and squeezed tightly. I wanted my grip to make his words untrue. I wanted the moment to disappear. Kamal hugged me while I had a terrible cry and he cried too. I threw up all my rainbow sweets onto the carpet. I had a nervous stomach and felt shaky. I was angry with God and wanted my father.

They told me everything would be fine, but I didn't think so. Nothing seemed like it would be fine ever again. For two days, I hardly spoke to anybody even though everyone tried to talk with me. I didn't know how to tell them that everywhere I went I thought I'd see my dad. I didn't know how to tell them that I felt alone. I cried in bed because he wasn't there to read me poems, and sing our song, and make life feel fine.

At the funeral service, we looked at Dad and said goodbye together - Kamal, Ramona, Maxwell and me. He looked peaceful sleeping in his suit.

"Go on you can do it," Ramona said to me.

Maxwell whispered, "Just be brave."

I leaned forward and gave my rainbow painting to him. I wanted my dad to be in the happiest place I could imagine.

"I know he really loves that!" Kamal said, smiling. And I loved it too.

Back in my seat, I felt safe and important listening to the reverend and everyone say super things about my dad.

After the funeral, many people came to my house. We had plenty of food and desserts to eat. All the children played together while the big ones took care of the younger ones. My family laughed and had a good time. I saw mommy laughing too! She looked beautiful in her red velvet dress, my dad's favorite color. She said she was proud of me for being mature during a difficult time. I did feel bigger and wiser. I told her I thought my dad was like a celebrity or superhero. It felt really good to say that. "To us he is," Mom said. "And he always will be."

It was a very sad time, but that day was sort of fun. I knew my dad was already an angel looking down on us because he always made people laugh and have fun. I could feel his love all around, and I knew in my heart that my life, this life, our life would be fine.

About the Author

Deardra Zahara Duncan, M.A., Ed.M, M.S.Ed. is a veteran educator, School Counselor, Certified Life Coach, Spiritual Advisor and proud mother of two. Her many years of work with children, teens and adults have been dedicated to nurturing healthy emotional development and healing. Her professional focus is directed towards helping people master social interactions and interpersonal relationships. This competence is achieved through guided exploration of one's own self-awareness, self-reflection, willingness to self-expand, forgive and love thyself. Mostly autobiographical, *Life is Fine*, depicts the beginning of Deardra Zahara Duncan's journey as a child through many family deaths, bereavement, traumas, and learning to have a positive outlook on life. Deardra Zahara Duncan is passionate about the role 'truth storytelling' plays in the ability to heal, transform, inspire, and enrich lives. Ms. Duncan lives in Jersey City and can be reached at her website.

About the Illustrator

Kalila Ain Abdur-Razzaq began her formal art education at the High School of Art & Design and The Art Students League of New York. She earned her Bachelor's degree in Painting and Art History from SUNY Purchase College and studied fresco restoration at Institute Lorenzo de' Medici in Florence, Italy. Kalila Ain is a figurative painter primarily working in oil, however she also favors watercolor, printmaking and collage. Kalila Ain holds two permanent installations at the Morgan Stanley Children's Hospital in New York City, and her painting 'The Renaissance Woman' resides in the permanent collection of The Colored Girls Museum of Philadelphia, PA. Kalila Ain is passionate about art's role and ability to heal, transform, inspire and enrich the world. Ms. Abdur-Razzaq lives in New York City and can reached at her website
www.kalilaabdurrazzaq.com

Special Note: *Life Is Fine* is the first book collaboration with Deardra Zahara and Kalila Ain, who are mother and daughter. They heal, transform, inspire and passionately enrich each other's lives daily.